US

forward:
RICK BARRY

Authors

**Robert Geline and
Priscilla Turner**

Photography

**Heinz Kluetmeier
Bruce Curtis
Martin Takigawa**

 RAINTREE EDITIONS

Published by   **Raintree Editions**
A Division of Raintree Publishers Limited
Milwaukee, Wisconsin 53203

Distributed by   Childrens Press
1224 West Van Buren Street
Chicago, Illinois 60607

Library of Congress Cataloging in Publication Data

Geline, Robert.
    Forward: Rick Barry.
    SUMMARY: A profile of Rick Barry, the "Golden Boy"
of the Golden State Warriors, based on interviews with
Barry, family, associates, and friends.
1. Barry, Rick, 1944-   —Juvenile literature.
2. Basketball—Juvenile literature. [1. Barry, Rick, 1944-
2. Basketball—Biography] I. Turner, Priscilla, joint author.
II. Curtis, Bruce. III. Kluetmeier, Heinz. IV. Title.
GV884.B3G44   796.32'3'0924 [B] [92]   75-42339
ISBN 0-8172-0123-8
ISBN 0-8172-0122- X lib. bdg.

Contents

Warm-up

Why is a winning basketball coach like a safecracker?
Answer: Because each of them must be able to find
the right combination.

Perhaps more than any other sport, basketball has to be a
team effort. It is great for a club to have a Wilt Chamberlain
or a Kareem Abdul-Jabbar or a Rick Barry. But it takes
all five on a team to play basketball with the consistency,
coordination, and sense of oneness that can win it all. In
professional basketball it takes an entire squad that can
do it together.

But just as a team must have the right combination, so must
an individual player. In order to be a winner, a star, he
must have all the right physical skills and mental attitudes
and emotional intensity.

This book is about a team that came together, that "clicked"
to make a championship season, and about the captain of
that team, whose life so far has been directed by his
athletic skills, his competitive drive, and his feelings about
himself, and how all these personal qualities combined to
make him an All-Star and a team leader in his sport.

That Championship Season

"... When it was over, I was so overcome with emotion, I just sat there and had a little cry."

The Golden State Warriors had just beaten the Capital Bullets for the fourth game in a row — this time by the score of 96-95 — to win the National Basketball Association championship for 1974-'75.

It was an incredible accomplishment. No one had given the team from Oakland, California, a chance for *any* success when the season began. But they had succeeded beyond anyone's dreams, even their own. They had put it all together. And the man who wept tears of joy when it was over was Rick Barry, the Warriors' captain.

His teammates had chosen him captain long months before, in October, when the grueling professional basketball season of nearly 100 games begins. The honor meant a lot to Barry. He had been playing basketball for more than 20 years—in grade school, high school, college, and the pros. He had always been a standout, acknowledged as one of the finest ever to play the game. But it was the first time he had ever been chosen captain.

The job was something he wanted. He had approached the season thinking the Warriors could do well — if the

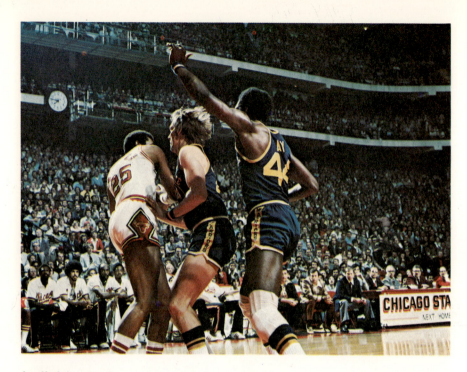

individual players worked together for team goals. Except
for Barry, almost all the Warrior stars of years past were
gone. Nate Thurmond, the huge center, had been traded
to the Chicago Bulls. The sharp-shooting Cazzie Russell
would be wearing the gold and purple of the Los Angeles
Lakers, the Warriors' arch rival. Rugged rebounding
Clyde Lee had been lost to the Atlanta Hawks.

A mix of young, untested first-year players and additions
from other clubs would try to make Warrior fans forget their
departed heroes. There were rookies Jamaal (Keith) Wilkes
— the smooth-playing forward from UCLA whose nick-
name was "Silk" — and Phil Smith, a high-leaping guard
from San Francisco. They looked like good prospects. There
was massive Clifford Ray, the bearded six foot nine inch
center the Warriors had obtained from the Bulls in the
Nate Thurmond deal. Ray was good, but few thought he
could take Thurmond's place. And there were others, like

Charles Dudley, who hadn't even played professional basketball the previous year. There was potential, but no one knew how much, or how good these new Warriors would become.

"I was pessimistic before the season began," says Rick. "I felt it was going to be a rebuilding year. I thought that by being captain I could both help some of the younger players and help my own attitude toward the game at the same time. And I thought that, by being captain and taking an active role, our team could progress to the point where we would cause some trouble for other teams and at least have an enjoyable season."

It became so enjoyable it made him cry.

The Warriors began the season with Rick leading them in scoring, in assists — just about everything anyone counts in basketball — and also to victory after victory. His

9

sensational performances were not surprising. Rick had been an established superstar for years, and could be relied on to score nearly 30 points every time he took the floor.

But the Warriors' winning ways were something else. With Barry playing the best basketball of his career, and the new players fitting into Coach Alvin Attles' plans like pieces of a jigsaw puzzle — that combination again — the Warriors comfortably led their division and had close to the best record of any NBA team as the league's annual mid-January All-Star game approached. Their record was 27 wins and 13 losses. Only the Baltimore Bullets had done better. Still, most believed the young, surprising team from Oakland wouldn't keep winning in the long second stage of the season.

For a while after the All-Star game, it looked as if these doubters would be right. Between mid-January and mid-March, the Warriors won 14 games and lost 17. Something had happened to the team. Their early season success had gone to their heads. They began to think they could win with good shooting and offensive play alone. Their defensive play was going downhill. Teams they had beaten badly before the All-Star game were now beating them.

Rick Barry is a bad loser. "Losing really eats at me," he says. "A lot of guys can take winning and losing in stride. A lot of guys couldn't care less. Well, I care." As team captain, he set out to do what he could to get the Warriors back on the winning track.

He had told his teammates when the season began that as captain, he would occasionally be telling them things about their play they might not like. "But I won't be doing it to put you down," Barry told them. "If I do criticize you, I will be doing it in a constructive way."

Now, at team meetings, Barry pointed out to his younger teammates that the Warriors were losing because they really

weren't as good as they had come to believe in their
successful season start. He reminded them that they had
to work hard for every win, and that playing good defense
together was the key to victory.

The message was heard. The Warriors found the combination again. When the regular season ended, they were
champions of their division. Their record was 48-34, fourth
best in the NBA. Barry's scoring average of 30.6 points per
game — second best in the league — was business as usual
for Rick. So was his league-leading free throw shooting
percentage of .904. Everyone knew Barry was a great scorer.
But the most surprising statistic, and the one that best
reflected his great all-around play, was his league-topping
average of almost three steals a game.

Ahead of Rick and the Warriors lay the championship
playoffs, professional basketball's second and most
important season. They were ready for the challenge.

They beat their first playoff opponent, the Seattle Supersonics, without much trouble. Next came the Chicago Bulls, a team that had given the Warriors a lot of trouble during the regular season. The Bulls were veterans who played a special brand of tough, aggressive, hard-driving basketball. The "smart" people thought the Bulls would end the Warriors' season by beating them handily in the playoff series.

It almost happened. The Bulls moved to within one victory of winning the series, and they looked like the stronger team. To keep their hopes alive, the Warriors had to beat the Bulls twice in a row. It seemed too much to hope for, but the Warriors did it, by scores of 86-72 and 83-79. In the final game against the Bulls, Barry led all scorers with 36 points.

The Warriors beat the Bulls because they had learned well their lesson about playing hard on defense in order to win. Twice they kept the Bulls from scoring for long periods in the second half of those two crucial games. That made the difference.

The one team now standing between the Warriors and the championship of the NBA was the Capital Bullets. The Bullets had the league's best record. They were a team of All-Stars: Elvin Hayes, Wes Unseld, Phil Chenier, Kevin Porter, Mike Riordan. The Bullets had beaten the Buffalo Braves *and* the Boston Celtics to win the right to meet the Warriors. The Celtics had been the reigning NBA champions, and the Braves a team that everyone agreed had the potential to be great. Both teams seemed as good as, if not better than, the Warriors. And the Bullets had beaten them. To ask the Warriors to beat the Bullets was to ask that an impossible dream come true.

It was over quickly, stunningly. The Warriors beat the Bullets four games in a row. They came from behind to win — as they had come from behind all season — in three of the four games. They beat the Bullets because they

13

played together as a team. They beat the Bullets because they played almost perfect defense when they had to. They beat the Bullets because each of them played brilliantly as an individual. Judged to be best of all in the series was Rick Barry, who was named the Most Valuable Player.

Rick had averaged 29.5 points per game for the series. He had hounded the Bullets on defense and made brilliant passes to his teammates for baskets. In the beginning of what was to be the final game, the Bullets' Mike Riordan actually grabbed Rick and wrestled him from behind as Rick was about to outrace Riordan to the basket. Warrior Coach Attles, furious, was thrown out of the game, but Barry was cool enough to ignore the attack and continued to "smoke" Riordan throughout the game.

Riordan's attempted tackle was the Bullets' final futile gesture. When the game was over, the Warriors were the champions of the NBA.

Barry certainly was proud of being named Most Valuable Player, but he was even prouder of his team. He pointed out how much better the Warrior substitutes had performed in the series than the Bullets' substitutes. Their scoring was much better in every one of the four games. The defense played by these substitutes was quick and tireless, and it drove the Bullets' guards to distraction.

Again, the message of success was team play, team spirit. Throughout the series the Warriors could be seen congratulating each other for good plays, good passes, and fine shots, and encouraging each other with cheers and signals. Players the crowd and the national TV audience had never heard of — Phil Smith, Charles Dudley, Derrek Dickey, George Johnson — created so much pressure with their fine play that the Bullets cracked, four straight times.

The tears that Rick shed after the final victory were proof that the dream had come true. And the tears were strong evidence that Barry was not a selfish, money-mad star who thought only of himself — as some had said — but a captain for whom his team's success was the peak of a life in basketball.

The Professional

Combinations are the secret of team success in basketball, and they also are the key to individual success. The combination of physical gifts and skills, desire, and persistence makes for superior athletes. Physical ability alone often isn't enough. Mental toughness and determination to stick to a task are even more important.

If professional athletes are different from most people, it may be in this determination and confidence. These are qualities that Rick Barry has, and he knows he has them.

"I just feel that I have proven that I am a complete player, and that I would have to be considered one of the best forwards who has ever played the game," Rick Barry says. "And that's all that really matters because 20 years from now, who's going to care? They'll be talking about somebody else."

Maybe and maybe not. Anyone who has ever seen Rick play will be a long time forgetting him. Every stolen ball, every lightning-like pass to an open teammate, every slashing drive past a dumbfounded defender for an easy layup, will keep Rick Barry in basketball fans' minds long after he has stopped playing. Many have praised his basketball ability, but maybe Rick has said it best: "One thing no one ever has to worry about — Rick Barry playing good basketball."

Such statements have helped make Barry one of the most criticized men in all professional sport. He has been called arrogant, a money-hungry man interested only in himself, because of his switch to the newly formed American Basketball Association just two years after he began playing pro ball. He has been labeled a hot dog because of his flashy wardrobe and razor-cut hair style. And he's been called a "gunner" and a "cry baby" because of his high scoring and on-court temper tantrums and arguments with officials.

Rick feels that he has been misunderstood by the press and the public. "I have always played for the team that had me under contract," and, "I've never denied the basketball to an open man," are two things he says to refute those who criticize him off the court and on it. He says it's only now, more than ten years into his professional career, that people are beginning to understand and accept what he's all about:

"I'm an intense and very emotional person — competitive, a perfectionist. I can't stand mediocrity in myself or other people." That attitude has helped make him an outstanding basketball player. But it hasn't always made him an easy person to like.

Rick thinks that he has his temper pretty well under control now. During his championship season with the Warriors, in fact, he was almost a model of on-court restraint. He says he even surprised himself at times. But what most people don't understand, Rick points out, is that his running battle with the officials has been as much a part of his game as his jump shot. Whenever he'd try to subdue the flashes of anger, he'd find that he just wasn't getting sent to the free throw line. "I went back to screaming," he says, "and I began to get my free throws again. It's a fact."

Rick is able to shrug off most of the criticism because he believes people mistake his confidence for cockiness. "There's a fine line between the two," he says. "A cocky person is someone who thinks he's good, but he's not. A confident person is someone who actually believes he can accomplish what he has set out to do. Any successful person, no matter what they're doing, has that type of confidence. It's necessary."

What wasn't so easy to shrug off were the harsh words — "disloyal money-grubber," "Joe Greed" — that were often hurled at him in the five years of his odyssey from the NBA to the new ABA and back to the old league. Rick was the first big-name player to switch leagues, joining the now defunct Oakland Oaks when he thought he would be teaming up with his former college coach (and his father-in-law), Bruce Hale.

In the middle of his second professional season with the Warriors, Rick was approached by representatives of the Oakland Oaks ABA franchise. The ABA was being formed, and its backers wanted young but proven NBA talent. At that point, Rick was having problems with Bill Sharman, the Warrior coach, whose computer-like, no-nonsense approach to basketball just wasn't Rick's style. "Under Bill Sharman," says Rick, "basketball was no fun."

The Oaks backers offered Rick partial ownership of the new team, a $75,000-a-year salary, and, most important, promised that Bruce Hale would coach the team. That clinched it for Rick. He probably could have gotten the same salary from the Warriors, but he opted for the ABA and a coach he liked.

Things went downhill after that. Because he was still under contract to the Warriors, Rick sat out the Oaks' first season. Without him, the team went on to the worst record in the league, losing 56 games and winning only 22. After that first season, Bruce Hale was replaced as coach.

The next year, the Oaks made it to the ABA playoffs. But Rick didn't. He was sidelined after 35 games with a bad knee injury that later led to the first of two knee operations he has had in his professional career.

One of the assurances Rick had received before he signed with the Oaks was that the team would stay in the San Francisco area. But after that second season in Oakland, the team was sold, and the new owner moved it to Washington, D.C., renaming it the Washington Caps.

Rick sued the new owner, citing breach of contract. That move was even more unpopular with fans than his switch to the ABA. The press sniped at him, saying he had made his bed and now he could lie in it.

Rick played with the Caps for one long season. His family was in faraway Oakland. Team spirit was nonexistent. For the first time, Rick was on a team where there was tension between white and black players. He was miserable, and ready to get back to the NBA. That would come, but not

before another stop in the ABA, this time to play for the New York Nets.

The ABA experience is one Rick wouldn't repeat. He hurt his knee and worried that the injury would shorten his career. He spent a whole season away from his family. It was hard on him and his wife, Pam. But Rick puts those years in perspective: "I've always believed that things have a way of working out for the best."

And there were some good things about those times. For example, while playing for the Nets, Rick was the host of a TV talk show. It was a first step toward the broadcasting career he wants to follow after his days as a player are over.

Rick's jump to the ABA is one good example of his individualism. A lot of people thought he was wrong to do it, but Rick followed his own mind. By consistently doing

that, he has gained a reputation as something of a trail-blazer in professional sports. It's a role he says he doesn't actively try to play. "I don't look to be the pioneer," he insists. "It just seems to be something that happens."

For example, there's his celebrated razor-cut hair style. It's now common for professional athletes to take special care of their hair and appearance. Rick Barry was one of the first to do that. As he tells it: "When I came to San Francisco, I got to meet a guy who was a barber. He was European and he did all these razor things. I thought that was great, so I started doing it — spending seven dollars and 50 cents for a haircut while everybody else was getting two dollar specials. I wasn't doing it to get publicity. It was just something I wanted to do, so I did it. Being the pioneer was the farthest thing from my mind."

Along with his exceptional skills as a basketball player, it is his knack for doing things a little differently off the court that makes Rick Barry a special man in professional basketball. As Roy Boe, owner of the New York Nets, says about him in the book, *Confessions of a Basketball Gypsy: The Rick Barry Story:* "Whatever else he is, he is, above all things, a star."

4

Growing Up

Richard Francis Barry III was born March 28, 1944, in Elizabeth, New Jersey, a port city just across the Hudson River from New York City. Elizabeth at that time was typical of many towns on the east coast. It was a true melting pot — a place where people of all races, religions, and nationalities lived. There were blacks and whites, rich and poor, Catholics, protestants, and Jews.

Alpha Barry and Richard Barry II, Rick's parents, also were born in Elizabeth. He was of Irish descent and her people were Lithuanian. When Rick was born, his father had a job with the Western Electric Company and made about 54 dollars a week. The family wasn't rich, but lived comfortably on the first floor of a two-story house.

Both Rick and his older brother Dennis — almost from the time they first walked — were sports minded and constantly on the go. Especially Rick. He was always outdoors playing some game. If it wasn't football, basketball, or baseball, it was stickball, tetherball, hide-and-seek, or ring-a-lerio — a kind of combination of cops and robbers and king of the hill. Rick didn't particularly care what game he played; he just wanted to play all the time.

Except when he got tired. One thing Alpha Barry never had trouble with was getting her youngest son to go to bed.

"My mother could never get over that," says Rick. "Most kids would do anything to stay up. But when I got tired, the President of the United States could have been sitting in our living room and it wouldn't have mattered. If I was tired I'd just walk in and say to everybody, 'Excuse me, I'm tired. I'm going to sleep.'"

Rick's judgment about getting the rest he needed was much better than the judgment he showed when his neighborhood friends suggested pranks. They pulled some pretty dangerous stunts. One of their favorite pastimes was hitching rides on the freight trains that ran through the city. The railroad detectives were always after them, but they rigged up an elaborate escape system and never got caught. Before going down to the railroad yard, the gang hung a cable down from a vacant lot above the tracks. When the detectives ran after them, Rick and his friends shinnied up the cable to safety, pulling it after them to make their getaway. Looking back, Rick figures he was pretty lucky not to get himself into a lot of trouble.

Rick started to smoke cigarettes when he was 12 years old. His older brother Dennis thought the kid was starting to "go bad." One day Dennis spotted Rick playing pinball, a cigarette dangling from his mouth. He dragged Rick away from the pinball machine, gave him a stiff lecture on smoking and how bad it was for someone who wanted to be good in sports, and worse, threatened to tell their parents. The threat worked. Rick stopped smoking.

Even though he didn't study hard, Rick did well in school. He was a bright child; his mother had received permission to enroll him a year early. Rick admits not liking books. He managed to get through by paying close attention in class. He has a very good memory. As an altar boy in church, he was always the first one to memorize his prayers, and he could recite them faster than anyone. He also found shortcuts for his class assignments. For example, he used to write book reports using Classic Comics. He'd infuriate his classmates by making all As and Bs. They couldn't figure out how he did it.

But there was nothing mysterious about his athletic ability, and sports were always Rick's first love. He had plenty of encouragement to practice and develop his athletic skills, too. His father had been a semiprofessional basketball player, and knew the game well. "I really learned the game and what the game is all about from my father," Rick says.

Rick's dad was his first coach. Barry, Sr., coached the team at Saints Peter and Paul, the school Rick and Dennis attended. Both of them played and learned the fundamentals of the game — passing, dribbling, shooting, defense — from their father. And the team won championships.

Now, when Rick gives pointers to beginning players at the basketball camp he runs during the summer, he repeats

what his father told him long ago: "The fundamentals of the game are as important to your future development as the foundations of a tall skyscraper. You put a weak foundation there, and you can only build so high before the building is going to topple over. It's the same way with basketball fundamentals. If you don't learn them, no matter how much God-given talent you have, you will never develop into a great basketball player."

Basketball wasn't Rick's only sport. Nor was it even his favorite. Baseball was his first love. The Giants, who played in New York when Rick was growing up, were his team. Willie Mays, a black man who wore uniform number 24, was his man.

Rick's dad taught him to catch fly balls with the basket-style catch that was the great Mays' special trademark. Rick loved to watch the Giants' centerfielder catching balls that way.

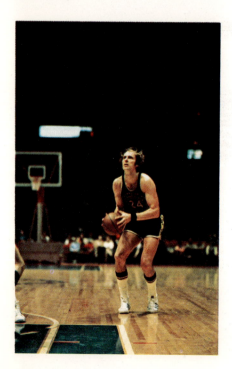

Rick once clambered over the wall from the stands at the old Polo Grounds, where the Giants played, to run out on the field and shake Willie's hand. That night at dinner, Dennis mentioned that he'd been watching the Giants game on television and had seen some kid, hotly pursued by stadium guards, run onto the field to meet Willie Mays. Since Rick had skipped school to go to the game, and didn't want anyone to know, he didn't admit he was that kid.

But Willie Mays remained his hero. That's why Willie's number, 24, has always been on Rick's basketball jerseys.

Getting Serious About Basketball

Rick's parents raised him to be independent and self-reliant. They wanted him to think for himself and learn to make his own decisions. That training really began to show when he went to Roselle Park High School. It was there that he decided to get serious about basketball — after he had a problem with a baseball coach.

Rick was a pitcher on the junior varsity team. But he also was a good hitter, and wanted to play another position in games he wasn't pitching. He was hitting .500 as a pitcher, and thought that he had a right to play before other kids who couldn't hit as well. But his coach had other ideas. Rick continued to ride the bench in games when he wasn't pitching. "So I told him to take the game and keep it," says Rick, "and I left. I got turned off to baseball and really concentrated on basketball from that point on."

Basketball became his whole life. Strange as it sounds, his teeth might have more to do with that than anything else.

Rick's permanent teeth came in while he was at Roselle Park. But his eyeteeth were missing, and the others came in crooked. "I thought I looked hideous," says Rick. "I just hated myself. I talked to people with my hand over my mouth, and I wouldn't look them in the eye. It had a horrendous effect on my personality. I pulled myself into this little shell

and got totally engrossed in basketball, because that was life for me then."

Rick had his teeth fixed when he was in college. But, says his wife Pam, "To this day, he still has a habit of talking out of the side of his mouth and not looking at somebody, and I'll say, 'Ricky, you can look at them now.' It must have been a hard thing for him to overcome."

Though self-conscious about his looks as a youth, Rick never went through a physically awkward stage, as so many tall people do when they're growing. Rick was always tall for his age, but he never was a freak. As a matter of fact, he was only six feet one inch tall as a high school junior. By the time he graduated, he was three inches taller. He grew to his full six feet seven and one-half inches in college.

Although Rick threw himself into basketball, his high school coach almost made him quit. Rick felt, and still does, that basketball, and all sports, should be fun. "But he made it like a job," says Rick, "and I didn't like that." He continued to play because he knew it was his chance to get a college scholarship. After one game, though, Rick was so discouraged that he came home in tears.

The coach hadn't liked the way the varsity had played in practice that week, so in the next game, he started the junior varsity instead. Rick was frustrated and mad. The coach finally sent him and his teammates into the game, when Roselle Park was losing by 31 points. They almost made up the difference, but wound up losing the game by a single point. That was the last straw. "I was ready to quit," Rick says. His family finally talked him out of it.

The Roselle Park team was never outstanding when Rick played there, but Rick was. In his senior year he was one of the best high school basketball players in New Jersey and was named to the All-State team. Although he was only 16 years old as a senior, and not as fully developed physically

as many of the other players, more than 30 colleges approached Rick with offers of athletic scholarships.

Liking his coach had always been important to Rick. He knew that wherever he went to college to play basketball, it was important that he play for a coach he liked and respected. Of all the coaches who wanted him to come to their schools, he liked Bruce Hale, the basketball coach at the University of Miami, the best. "He took an interest in me as a person," says Rick.

And so, although his parents wanted him to stay closer to home, Rick headed south for four more years of basketball. It was to be much more than that.

Miami

Rick calls his decision to go to the University of Miami, Florida, "the one perfect move" he's made in his life. Everything about Miami appealed to him—the sunshine, the beaches, the basketball coach—even the coach's daughter, Pam. But that discovery came a little later. Rick went to college to play basketball. Although he says he wouldn't have gone to a school that had a poor academic reputation, he also admits: "I went to college to play basketball and get an education." In that order.

After all, basketball was the most important thing to him and, he hoped then, his future meal ticket. Above all, in picking his college, he wanted a coach he liked and respected. Bruce Hale, the basketball coach at Miami, was that man.

Hale offered Rick a full scholarship, but without the frills many coaches offer to attract top-notch players—no cars, clothes or extra money. He received his room and meals, books, tuition, and 15 dollars a month for laundry. Rick's parents didn't have much to give, but sent him 10 dollars whenever he wrote home, usually about once a month.

Miami didn't give out many basketball scholarships, so each player who got one knew he would have a good chance to play a lot of ball. That really appealed to Rick. "Bruce let you know that, if he felt you were good enough, you were

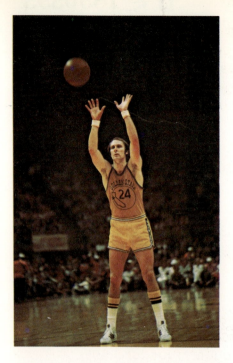

going to play. He didn't bring in 15 or 20 guys on scholarships and have a war out there on the floor to see who made
the first team," says Rick.

Rick worked hard and it paid off. As a freshman, he
averaged 28 points a game. Not known as a hard worker in
practice as a pro, he spent countless evenings practicing
alone in the gym at Miami.

He didn't just practice shooting. Rick feels that an
outstanding player must do everything well. So he practiced
everything — faking, tipping the ball against the basket,
shooting, dribbling, moving without the ball, and, of course,
the devastatingly accurate underhand free throw technique
his father had taught him. It is a free throw style that was
used by most players in the 1930s.

Such devotion to basketball didn't leave much time for
anything else. What spare time Rick had was spent at Bruce
Hale's house swimming, talking, or just relaxing. Most of

the players congregated there. Rick's happiest college memories are of the times he spent at the Hale home. Pam Hale, the coach's daughter, was an added attraction for Rick. She was only 15 years old when they met in Rick's freshman year. But he was young, too — 17, a year younger than most of his classmates.

Pam had grown up around basketball players. "From the time I was nine years old," she says, "I was always the mascot of the team."

Pam's mother, Doris Hale, had picked Rick up at the airport when he first arrived in Miami. She took a liking to Rick right away. He didn't smoke or drink, and his manners were good. He reminded her of a little boy who needed mothering, tall and skinny with a crew-cut and pants that were too short. She told her daughter about him.

But when Pam met Rick, it was anything but love at first sight. She thought he was arrogant, rude, and ugly on top of it. For his part, Rick was sarcastic to Pam and teased her mercilessly about being "a high school kid." But then came a movie Rick took Pam to as payment for a lost bet. To her amazement, he was nice to her the whole evening. There was not one sarcastic remark about Pam being a mere high schooler. "Rick was different from any college boy I ever went out with because he was so serious," remembers Pam.

Rick admits that he was serious, but not so much about Pam or school as about basketball. He and Pam dated steadily, and Rick maintained a B average, good enough to get him elected to the honor society. But basketball was his first priority.

He improved tremendously each year at Miami. In his junior year he really hit his stride and began to get the national attention that has been his ever since. He averaged 32 points and 16 rebounds a game, making a couple of

All-American teams in the process. He tried out for the 1964 Olympic team, and was bitterly disappointed not to be chosen.

It was during his college days that he came to be known as a player with a hair-trigger temper, a reputation that has plagued him ever since. "It's only taken about ten years for me to get the temper under control," says Rick.

One incident that helped build that reputation occurred in Rick's junior year, during a big game against Loyola of the South. Rick, continuously harassed by one Loyola player, started to give back what he had been getting. As the game progressed, the tension between them increased. Finally, when they went up for a jump ball, the Loyola player smacked Rick in the face. As they came down, Rick wheeled around and returned the blow. The other guy went down with a broken jaw and fractured cheekbone and was carried away, unconscious. Rick regretted the incident, but didn't think he was wrong.

But the story doesn't quite end there. On his way to the hospital to apologize to his opponent, Rick unthinkingly stopped to pick up a box of candy. The gesture was there, but you don't take a box of candy to someone who's in the hospital with a wired jaw, particularly if you are the one who broke it! "There are times when I don't believe myself," says Rick. But the injured player wasn't bitter about the incident. "It's not everyone who can say he's had his jaw broken by Rick Barry," was his comment.

Rick's terrible temper didn't always endear him to the fans or his coach, and certainly not to the referees. Nonetheless, his temper was a reflection of his competitive drive and, somehow, the madder he got the better he played. Alex Hannum, who was to be Rick's first professional coach, watched Rick play in an AAU tournament that included the Russian national team. Even though it wasn't an important championship, Rick was playing as if his life depended on it. It was the end of the season and he was exhausted. The Russian team was giving Rick lots of abuse, but, Hannum remembers, "When Rick got mad it made him better, not worse. I could see he was something special." Hannum later told Rick that he decided to draft him on the basis of that game.

In his senior year at Miami, Rick averaged 37 points and 18 rebounds a game. He played 17 games in which he scored 40 or more points. In six of those games he scored at least 50 points. Rick was the leading college scorer in the country, racking up a total of 973 points for his senior year, and 2,298 points for his college career. He was picked on the All-American teams and was chosen to play in the East-West All-Star game.

The pros were taking a hard look at him. His talent was undeniable. But the scouts weren't sure he could success-fully make the transition from college ball to the bone-

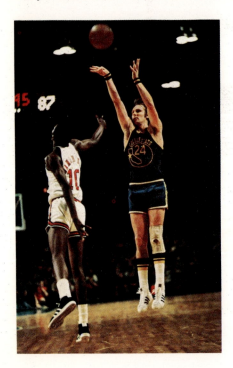

crunching style of the NBA. Rick was called "skinny" and "too flaky," a reference to his temper tantrums on the court.

During the 1964-1965 NBA season, the San Francisco Warriors had finished at the bottom of their division, so they had their pick of the graduating seniors. The Warriors' front office swallowed hard and made Rick Barry a first-round draft choice. An All-Star pro's career was begun.

There was another special event for Rick that spring. He and Pam had grown serious about one another. Throughout college, she was the only girl he had dated steadily. They became engaged on Pam's birthday, December 30, in 1964. On June 12, 1965, right after Rick graduated, they were married. She was 19 years old and he was 21.

At Camp

Rick Barry stands at center court, a basketball cradled in his hands. Seated in a semicircle around him are 300 children, ages 9 to 13. There are black kids and white kids, Chicano and Asian-American youngsters, children of all sizes and shapes. They have come from all over northern California to learn about basketball as Rick Barry plays it, at a summer camp held at Sonoma State College.

One of the crowd is Richard Francis Barry IV, whom everyone calls Scooter. Scooter is the oldest of Rick and Pam Barry's five children. This year, for the first time, he's participating in his dad's camp. But although he's Rick's son, Scooter is just one of the kids. Like everyone else, he's spending the week living in one of the dormitory rooms on the college campus.

You might expect the children of a basketball star to be stuck-up or something. But Rick and Pam have worked hard to help their kids keep a sense of perspective. "The boys are always around basketball and they love it," Rick says. "John and Scooter worked as ball boys for the Warriors last year. That was a real kick for me—to turn around during a time out and get a drink or a towel from one of them. But in fact, it was no big thing to them. I'm not even their favorite player."

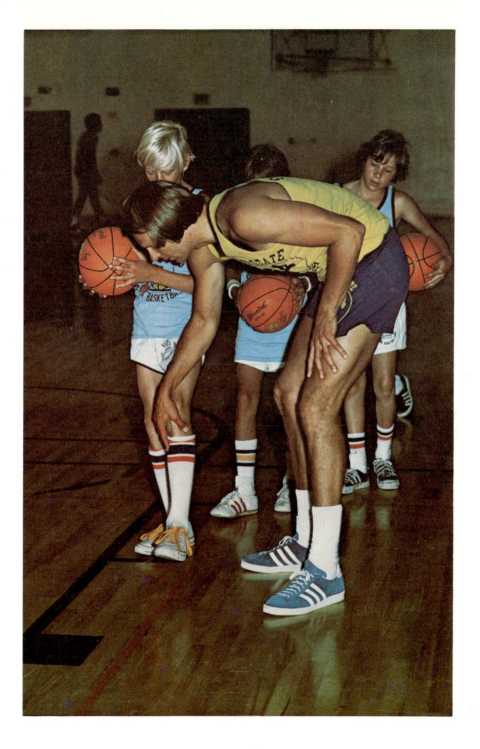

For the record, Rick points out that his three-year-old son Grant "loves Clifford Ray." "Somebody asked him who is in your family and he said, 'I have my brother Scooter, and John, and Drew, and Shannon, and Clifford Ray.'" Adds Pam, "It just seems that up to now our kids think it's neat that their father is a basketball player, but they don't think it's anything special, or that they're special because of it."

Like the other campers, Scooter is listening attentively to his dad's talk on the fundamentals of shooting a jump shot.

"Hold your hand directly beneath the ball so that the ball rests in the pad of your hand," Rick is saying. "That's the area between the palm of your hand and the tips of the fingers. You should put your hand out straight and let the ball rest comfortably on it.

"The next step is to turn your hand so that the hand is in a shooting position," Rick tells his listeners, raising the ball over his head, "without putting your other hand on the ball. In order to do that you have to cock your wrist properly so that the back part of the hand is at least parallel to the floor. Otherwise, the ball will fall off."

During the week, Rick will be watching the youngsters practice and play. From time to time, he'll step in to help someone with some aspect of the game — shooting, defense, rebounding. When the week is over, they'll have learned a lot about basketball, and also have had a lot of fun.

The fun part of the camp is important to Rick. "We try to organize the camp so that the kids enjoy themselves," he says. Along with games in the evenings, the kids watch special basketball movies and drill hard on the fundamentals Rick stresses during the day.

"The next important fundamental of the jump shot is to make sure that you have the arm holding the ball from the elbow to the wrist tucked in under the ball as straight as

possible," Rick continues. "You can't let your elbow drift out away from your body when you're shooting."

Three hundred listeners are paying close attention. Many have dreams of becoming basketball stars like Rick. Chances are good that none of them will make it, and Rick and the camp's coaches and staff have been quite candid in telling the campers that. But they also tell the kids that the lessons about working hard and practicing what they're learning apply to more than just basketball. Rick tells them to work hard in school as well as on the basketball court. He tells them to take care of their minds as well as their bodies—to avoid smoking and, above all, to stay far away from drugs.

"The last important fundamental of the jump shot is the follow-through. After you've released the ball at the top of your jump, try to put your index finger through the basket.

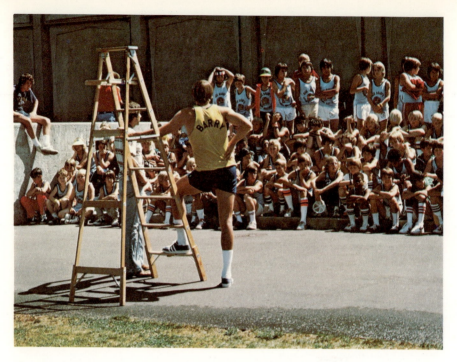

That's the way to make sure you get a good follow-through on the shot."

The lecture is over. The kids break up into teams and go off with their coaches to work on passing, dribbling, defense, shooting — all the fundamentals of the game that Rick Barry learned so well as a youngster. Rick watches the drills closely. At one point, he steps in to show someone how to shoot a layup from the left side of the basket. "You were here last year," he tells the youngster; "you should have learned that by now." He gives another kid a few pointers on defense: "The reason your man got behind you is because you turned your head and watched the ball. Now, try it again."

Watching him at camp, one wonders if Rick Barry has any interest in coaching when his playing days are over. Rick's answer is a flat "no." Coaching is not something he would enjoy, like the basketball camp.

And so it will go throughout the week. Lots of basketball and lots of fun. In many ways, the camp is a reflection of what Rick Barry thinks basketball, and life, should be all about. A perfect combination.